In Retrospect

In Retrospect

Elly Niland

First published in 2002
by Dido Press, an imprint of Aeneas Ltd

PO Box 200
Chichester
West Sussex
PO18 OJW
United Kingdom

© 2002, Elly Niland

Typeset in Bembo
by Marie Doherty

Printed and bound by
MPG Books
Bodmin
Cornwall
United Kingdom

ISBN: 1-902115-31-7

British Library Cataloguing in Publication Data
A catalogue record of this book is available from the British Library

Niland, Elly

For Chris (with love since St Patrick's day Wimbledon 17/03/1971), and for Philip, Paul & Matthew Niland.

Elly Niland was born in Guyana in 1954, and has lived in Surrey with her husband and children since 1971.

After studying as a mature student at Hillcroft College in Britain, she went on to read for her Modern Arts degree at Kingston University and then to take her PGCE.

Her time is now divided between teaching and working on a second collection of poetry. Elly is also writing an adaptation from a short novel for BBC Radio 4.

Acknowledgements

With much gratitude to Philip Niland, the editor of this first collection, for his surgical skill, and for his encouragement, vision and patience.

To my mother Veronica Prasad, for contributing the poem 'My Morning Star', and for her blessings.

Contents

To everything there is a season, and a time to every purpose under
  heaven:
A time to be born, and a time to die;
A time to plant, and a time to pluck up that which is planted;
A time to kill, and a time to heal;
A time to break down, and a time to build up;
A time to weep, and a time to laugh;
A time to mourn, and a time to dance;
A time to cast away stones, and a time to gather stones together;
A time to embrace, and a time to refrain from embracing;
A time to get, and a time to lose;
A time to keep, and a time to cast away;
A time to rend, and a time to sew;
A time to keep silence, and a time to speak;
A time to love, and a time to hate;
A time of war, and a time of peace.

Ecclesiastes 3:i–viii

Part 1

Lament

I think of you as young conscripts
Entering marriage
Without training or weapons.

In memoriam *Suzette Sabrina*

I   *Life Seeping Away*

Blinded with hope we journeyed in profound silence;
A procession of us at night
In menacing fog
To the intensive care unit where you lay.

Crawling past Salisbury Cathedral, panic threaded through.
Hope scattered, moon swelled
In gauze clouds against black cotton wool night.

Voices calling out to a sibling dying out.
Her fingerprints on the bedroom walls at home
Forming a sooty tapestry.
The last image of shred and bloom.

Minds reaching out. Sub-verbally. Unaware
Of the enormity of the tragedy which lay ahead.

II   *Breathless*

Our sister, curled up into a ball of submission,
Resembled a foetus, wrapped in its umbilical cord.
She withdrew into the core of her body
And crouched there.

She never did wake.

At 1:25am, you died.
Halted on the carousel of life,
Your last breath drifted like a veil.

III A Vacuum Of Time

Your head on a pink satin-lined bed,
A picture on the wall of a ship under sail.

A muddle of family
Stared into coffee as if there were messages in it.

Time between death and funeral
So like a badly edited film. Flickering.
A constant loop, running in the head.

Scenes repeat themselves,
But the sequence is all wrong.
Too many flashback frames.

Lurching, groping through time. Silence drips.
Nightmare and reality are inseparable.
Unable to regulate the mental clock.
Unable to find a brief moment
To nurse the pain. Or an
Even briefer moment
To forget it.

Body bags block up the paths to the brain.

IV Hand In Hand With Lakshmi:
Our Young Sister, Heading On Before

Watching wordlessly, shallow breathed,
Box closed like book.
Hearts thundered in chests as you
Descended slowly.

Ash and cinders. A smoky furnace.
You vanished in the grey-white-dust-storm
And brought to light
New words.

Death reached out with carnivorous intent.
And you ceased to be.

The Funeral

Your coffin chosen,
Burgundy silk clothes bought,
Poem and eulogy written.

Ready, aged 34 to be carried by your family out of
    church.
Such a sad convoy that day walking on shifting sand.
Parents shaking, covered you in petals.
Prayed for miracle but you didn't rise.
The Ave Maria was sung for your daughter,
Hymns chosen by all to shepherd you to a safer place.

All Saints Day today.
Feels now that you're missing.
A mixture of sickness and sorrow.

Your red dress and make up remain in Kingston.

So many tearful phone-calls overseas.
Gestures and obligations
Wistfulness then dread.

Death is now a condition of living
With peaceful periods between
Other catastrophes and paranoia.

Death certificates and plot numbers. Hallucinations.
Sunshine and haze and water cascades.
No machinery to repair except acceptance.

Posthumous Wonder

Comfort is elusive.
Cannot blast your way out of tragedy
Cannot turn down the sound
Cannot adjust images, cannot switch off.

Our roots are a long way from the surface now.

Winding paths through named roses.
Clouds scudding through sky.
Graveyard is a place of enclosure,
A vast mass of goodbyes.

A Decision to Re-Embrace Christ

We who are left behind live against our will:
We are not allowed to commit suicide;
We cannot impose pain on parents and kin.
We who have open wounds surrender our joy,
Hide in the dark. Coagulate. Boil.

Oh, elusive Death.

Daylight dawns, jagged and colourless.
Our children, the stars, light now.
They are the bright, glowing amongst scars.
In need of unconditional love and support.
The raison d'être.

Spacious

Mason.
Grave marks. Symbols of human fragility.
Evocative ties with past generations;
Mounds of spoil guarded and caretakered;
Neatly mown lawns of ruin.

Conservation.
Heritage centre, car parks and chapel. Paths cut and
    walked,
Everyone laid out tidily in lush colourful decay.

Preservation
Treasures, trees, surveyors, sites.
Historic monuments. Immovable.
Quarry-stone, marbles, cement stabilised.

Cracks filled in.

God made his statement; laid down his terms.
But is this sometimes a place of celebration?
Do people embrace and fly free?

Lilies and Roses for Mummy

Two daughters dead, and the mother's
Mad with dismay.
The SS Diamond and SS Latiff,
Her ships wrecked, in choppy seas
Hands rapt in rosary beads.

A life of premonitions, and
Long, long journeys to graves.

Life is now to be endured.
Hearts burnt abroad,
On greedy foreign soil for so many decades.

To look through her eyes you'd see,
Multiplied images of hearses and coffins
Descending. Yellow chrysanthemums
Red roses, pink buds, wreaths, bouquets
Flower baskets. Strains of hymns
Kaleidoscoped.

Closing Down

Faith and love combination,
She's shaping a means to an end.

Sensation,
Motivation, exploration,
All lost to you
Now that life's irretrievable.

You mourned your own going from Christmas to
    February;
A private grief and passion deep.
Architect in flux. Then triumphant
Enumerating. Inhaling. Anticipating.

The Dark, The Light, The End

Dark froth tickling tresses of your hair
Foaming death, collapsing wave.

Struggle to touch, to hold, to pray
Struggle towards the moment of exit.
Struggle to poison the heart of the matter
Teeth biting lips.

Momentary flashes, memories disappearing.
Bubbles, ceilings, ripples. Shining.
Blinded by the light.

A lake of souls departed, rows past
On schedule.
Hippocampus rises to dim all consciousness.
See The Lady of the Dance now,
Dimming mind groping.
Sightless eyes, lids wide open.
Cruising into God's sanatorium.

Untitled #44

She was thin and frail, with wavy brittle hair.
She emptied the bottle, draining it of clear fluid:
Reality slaked, poverty quenched. The trap is empty now.
Pot. Snaps shut.
Ripples and disappears.

Irreplaceable and Immovable
(Brampton Chapel—Ontario)

Huddled together, bundles of beings
In dejection and translucent light,
Shovelled like clean snow into
Gleaming long black car. Doors open—

Body refuses to move.
Silence a shade too dark.

In all this black and white
Red roses decorate you.
This is a Grimm's Fairy Tale nightmare on a bright day.

Wish for this blizzard to blind us, or postpone this
     moment for ever.
Valiantly we mop and dab water,
Bodies stiff with sadness.

We watch and wait.
Hearts straining to scream goodbye but angry race ensues.
Fractious fit, lidded eyes, thunderous noise in ears.

The cruelty of cremation is savage.
Ignition. Coffin sinking down.
Thoughts fall apart.

Unfathomable

The straits between us are irrational.
There'll be Christmas cards "Across the Sea"—no more.
This bitter salty water, so full of red herrings,
And full with metal shards.

November winds fierce within the mind are stinging.
Language communicates no more.
Night and day, water flows down hill.
Curtain calls of tears from incontinent eyes go
    unanswered.

Seasons of pain remain.

We remember your young eyes, mesmerized,
Like ripe black olives in a low moon.

The Texture of Existence

The emotion was sadness.
Mind strained at the edge of hysterical breakdown.
You just needed to take a rest from life.
To reassess.

I understand now your sense of paranoia,
Your sense of personal suffocation.
That calm was out of reach.
I understand that now ... in retrospect.

In Retrospect

You slumped on a sofa-bed.
Dead.
Motionless.

I understand now you were stalked by frustration.
Cordoned off. Consumed by contempt.

Mind closing down. Fog. Ebb. Mute.

Your absence is visible.

Editorial

No tutorial system designed by a human could
Teach good manners to acid tongues.
Flints. Stinging
Flashes of monosyllabic condescension.
Pyramids and speculation like:
> *"I didn't think that lightning would strike twice."*
> *"You must be paying for the sins of a previous life."*

And   *"Time's a great healer."*

How hard voices echo.

Inhibited

You *should* practice the art of the glad hand.

And yet those bereft by suicide must endure
Guilt and anger.
And for the mother an intolerable sense of rejection.

Kant, Rousseau, Hume, Thomas Aquinas, Dante.
You men. You give me nothing;
Taste/ethics/moral code/Essential selfishness/Shit.

Deep breaths,
Count to ten.
The end.

P.S. There is some connectedness surely …

Gravestones arranged as closely as words,
Multi coloured, like a panel of jurors lined up, ready
To pass sentence.
There are so many snatches of verse etched in columns
    long and short,
That we walk between the lines of an anthology in stone.

Thinking it Over

Graveyards sit on my shoulder
Like a malevolent bird of prey.

I marvel at the enormity of your plans.
Such a blazing shame.

You always had a sense of style, girls.
A taste for tragedy; intense, hard, heavy drama.

Now we just stare at each other in silence.

Four brown eyes closed for ever.
No wrinkles, no streaks of grey hair. No grandchildren.
No more extravagance, or lofty notions. No more fun.

The Murmuring

Streams of reminiscence, remembered, recalled,
Pictures roll over like leaves in Fall.
Thoughts and tears fall to the floor, like dead things.

You boxed up like rigid missiles.
Masks turned mournfully, helpless in your direction.
Upset and anger, a vague physical pain years later.

Birthdays bring portraits in and out of relief,
Fusion of this brings profound disbelief.
Life is one long act of disloyalty.

The Cemetery

Engraved slabs, vaults, some ornate.
Wrought iron gates gape wide.
Journey's end. Dug graves.
Only invertebrates venture forth from earth pried loose.

My Morning Star
by Veronica Prasad

A thousand prayers I whispered for you
Like tiny wings sent into empty space.
A million memories of your face
Haunt me as I pretend that you are there,
As though the golden link that binds
You to me is not broken.
A fountain of love like a little Kaieteur
Flows forever.
Secrets that we shared, words of love
And care
That were spoken
Still remain locked within me.
Glittering diamonds precious and rare,
Just like the ones that are asleep
Beside the Kaieteur,
To take wing, like my prayers
And to live by the shore of the
Fountain of my love forever more.

Part 2

Learning to See

The Going

I ordered a kilo of "unprecedented syntactical subtlety".
And now I'm just waiting for clarity of expression.

Oh, but what fun the ambiguities!
Fruitfully, happily they drop from the nib,
Fall at times and fly away.
Persistently though, some words hold on, clinging, staying,
Only to abandon you as you write.

When they stay, they crawl, float, like insects,
Some winged, flying
Digging, stinging.
For those that escape, you rummage like a beggar in a bin.

Half remembered words.
In transit.

The Storm Abates

Today I'm high. Three pieces folded and unfolded.
Happiness hangs in the air.
No leaves, no waves, no dust gathers.

Bid good bye to thundering sea, driftwood, and perils of
   the deep.

Fireworks soar, words fly upwards and sparkle clean;
Shiny streams against darkening skies.
No embers today, no flickering flames, no glow;
Part of the crowd once more.

Now I welcome little breakers against the shore,
And the first rays of the sun that sparkle on the dew.
I'm fishing from the recesses of an infertile mind.

The Thaw (Remembrance Sunday)

Copper beeches, foggy Thames
Frost hard and bright.

Birds sit fluting
Sad recurrent notes.

Sun parts cloud unexpectedly,
Warmth flutters over, panic recedes.

Stoke the embers with
A delicious sense of delinquency.

Unbidden memories flicker into consciousness.
Ashes in the fire glow.

A spell is cast,
Sentence staggers unsteadily.

Lilies are fragrant again.
In the still balmy air, silence is reviving.

Moored and buoyed up.
The sun shone with promise, bright and brief.

Poethood (1st Gear)
Writing School—An Eye Witness Account

She...   It's a craft.
Whilst writing, you must aim for economy and simplicity.
You must be precise, yet subjective.

Me...   Tall order: To be constructive against such heavy
odds.

She...   You need to possess a higher truth for the poetry
trade.
Truth, like surgery, hurts but cures.

Me...   OK. I'll just be Corbeau, the crow, the scavenger.

She...   You must embalm the odour of some memories.

Me...   What! The stench of death?

She...   Listen carefully. Detach yourself deliberately.

Me...   To leave irreconcilable fragments.

She...   Same time same place ...

But, I'm not a missionary, I have no zeal.

And so weeks pass in procrastination.
Red wine blurs vision.
And I give up with good-byes wreathing my mouth.

Museum in the Head

DAY 1
She, in anticipation packed her smile, toothbrush and
     pants,
Looking forward to a few days in the sun.
Clean air. New moon.

DAY 2
Arriving there, in spite of the maid service, the pool,
Breakfast on the veranda to the view of sea and hills …
     this luxury …
Her mind travelled backwards, discarding that radiant
     smile.

DAY 3
The purge began. The pen nib sang.
A splurge of nouns … a jam.
Lying sleepless, prey to words.
Congested thoughts disturbed.

DAY 4
Wind whipped up cerebral frenzy.
She lost herself
Exorcising words.

DAY 5
Dismasted ship drifting toward dawn.
Demand for words and wine diminished.

Mental Indigestion

To make the bread of life:
Take two pounds of flour, an ounce of salt,
And a slab of margarine. Mix together
With yeast and a bottle of claret, for fun.
Then peel the pages of a tragedy,
And stir in with a generous handful
Of sun-dried dreams.

Bake on gas-mark 5 for 3 days.
Eat with pay cheque in hand, triumphant.

Movement #41

Experience is not what happens to a man,
it is what a man does with what happens to him.

(Aldous Huxley)

Some party, somewhere.
Congregate mutely.
Keep your smile plastered. Laugh obligingly.

Gestures, effortfully expressed.
Forced to draw upon reserves
Which lay below the surface.
Words crawl out.
Prepare to say unpalatable things.

Recording is not a pleasing indulgence.
Words dance in and out, again and again and again,
Springing from the dark.

Lost summer, lost love, lost time.
Light's too bright.
And flowers exaggeratedly alive loom.

Poethood (2nd Gear)
"About Your Right To Relate…"

Writing words only turns speech into silence;
Blurs life into death,
And so reality dwindles.
The edges of unrelenting thoughts dissolve.

This writing of stuff is joyless and hopeless;
All that flight into fantasy … casting and recasting
    yourself,
Maybe you just need a wilful extinction of personality.

All the letters are barbed.
The alphabet bursts in deep detonations.
Such a deluge of anger and chaos,
You feel as if you're suffering from the bends
In the immersion of life.

But I have a grim determination to continue.
It's about motive and value.
So let the clichés fall on fallow ground.
And I'll write slowly, celibate and sober.

Poethood (3rd Gear)

Words tumble,
Waves break,
Memory bangs outside your head.

Dreaming, sleeping experimentally,
Pulse behind eye throbs rhythmic beat.

At last spell breaks, and
Muse descends to lots of laughter.

Choirs of words hum,
As first futile couplets invade the silence.

One year later. Stunned. No sweat, no wine, aloof and
    inaccessible.
Detached, weary, dichotomies displayed. Dying days and
Words and schizophrenic profiles ache as
Overtones of madness fuse. An antidote is overdue.

Books, flowers, music, ambrosia.
Mine.

Vegetative Interior Verbalisations of the Labouring Wordsmith

Millipede, centipede, segmented insects
Like errors
With fiendish ability to reproduce themselves.

A litter of paper
Ash trays full
Wine bottles empty

End of century
Fervent disbelief.
Hollow.
Strength needed only to work and conform
Pray only for sunshine

Circle fell apart, take apart, are apart.
When mothers lose children only a fraction of the iceberg is
Visible.
Senses numbed.

Suicide, terrible, incredible.

Poethood (4th Gear)

Significant Emissions

Distraught with passion,
I've retired now, pen dried after 21 months.
But I didn't feel a new sense of maturity.
Yesterday is just like today or tomorrow.
I rage. Still. I'm susceptible. I have the same faith and lack
   of it.

Strokes and curves are not witty, well informed or
   poignant.
I lack judgement, make hideous errors, write only
Banal repetitive words. Still,
I would have loved to have inherited the bold syntax gene,
And won on the lottery of literary landmarks, and
Moved towards a fuller understanding.

Still. Despite peaks and ruptures, aspiration swells.
It's an unvarying procedure you see:
Laying, playing, rising and toppling. Thoughts will march,
Splashing visions on the beach

This new voyage is a solitary one
No conversation, only dispensation.
Hours of vacuity, and selfish solitude,
Sketching a variety of diaphanous personalities,
In tones and notes cyclical.

Sea Nymph

The sea nymph is a nimble muse. She glides,
Prances on the seaweed, and rocks, convulsed with
  laughter.
She ripples.
Her features assail. Still.
Just now I saw her.
Changeless, outstretched and glossy. She sunned herself,
Spread her foamy form and sparkled liquid happiness.

Part 3

Picture Gallery

Tooting Market

(For Sandra—Sheherazade 1958–1997)

Should you dare for a smell and taste of home
Go to SW17 to the Sunday morning market:
See the ladies wearing bands of gold, smelling of nutmeg
    and thyme;
They sell nenwa, bora, bara and milky cassava.
You can try gulgula, awara, and guava.

In one tiny shop, you can buy salt-fish,
Pig-tail, plait-bread, star-fruit,
Tennis- rolls and coolade, golden-apple and foo-foo too.
Water-lilies and young frangipanis, maiden-hair ferns
And oleander—so vivid. Leaves you riveted. Wondering.

Senses intense; music, a poetry of colourful voices.
The variety is infinite. You can cry and laugh at once.

Men drinking Banks beer study the ladies. Glances
    skidding,
They stare absorbed, preoccupied, "speculating".
One to another said, "Boy, I might have a chance". His
    wife
selling banga-mary, hassa, huri and gilbaker overheard:

She was explicitly irreverent—to hoots of laughter;
She shouted to the crowd that her husband was a
    "misbegotten dilemma".
One hundred earnest smiles ensued and then they all
    applauded.
She then described his small "pointer broom," "a pencil
    without lead," she said
"…his crown jewels all lost."

Ochro and eddo, pigeon peas and sweet potato sold hot.
With such warmth.
Black pudding or pepper pot? Or souse? "Tek yuh time,
na rush. Pick and choose,"
Deliberate reasoned decisions to make. You see.
Such liberation. Such collaboration. Such loud laughter.
People walking side by side
Together.
On Sundays.

Thanks for the memory.

For Suzy

The last time we walked out of Craven Road together
She said:
"I am Queen banana with soft juicy layers of stem,
and waxy leaves.
From my heart grows the hand
Forming fruit.
I am that crimson flower,
I am the ratoon, the sucker from the old root.

I am hard King sugar cane,
The hurricane, cyclone and typhoon,
The heavy swell at sea.

I am Guyana, the land of water,
I am bauxite and diamonds
Sweet coconut water and its jelly.
I am the lily family and greenheart wood.
I am Rima, the perpendicular drop on Konawaruk.

I am, and
You are."

Berbice High School

Sound of the cane, hissing high in air
Before it descends on small brown hand
Stretched out full length.
Stomach churning, eyes burning,
The crack sounds on bare flesh.

Wince as wild cane bites into skin,
Pointless to beg for mercy.
Won't cry.

Goose flesh creeps down arms and legs,
Marks swell on palm of hand.

The fury of the lashes, the rage in his face.
Treated like wild dog, by brutal, practised sadist.

Learning without meaning, without happiness. 10 years old.
Degraded. D graded.

Fled.
Never to return.

Lunch on the South Bank

Smooth, glossy, delicate miniatures
Long to kiss them, mischievous kittens
Bathed with a radiance like opalescent jewels. Polished.
Brightness unveiled.

Some unwholesome food called "greens" were served:
Their eyes became opaque, then concentrated.
Tears reigned as upright principles were upheld.

All four needed the urinal urgently.
And there they slandered vegetables. In commotion.

With mental hygiene, adults carelessly misread innocence.
Our words collide.

Spent days slip away. Only fragrance remains.
Talking, eating and playing. Love lived in those three
    hours.
Remedies. Rays. Beautiful compositions:
Ben and Fenton, Ruana and Jethro.

For Anjuli Yuen-Tung
(who will be 7!)

She arrived in England,
This bright confetti five year old.

Cheery laughs and big hugs, a voice like fresh breeze.
(You'll dread the leaving afterwards so cling to these
  scenes.)

Alone, she entirely lifts the gloom, a lantern
In a room. A springtime blossom, anytime.

Sometimes if you mention bath time though,
There is loud irreverent indignation.
And the little monster scampers away.

Reya's candid daughter!
Playing games in earnest,
And watchful of her toys.

At 6:13 am this wide-awake energetic girl,
Surveys the breakfast cereal with unsurpassed fascination.
An old aunty needs wisdom, courage and patience.

So memorable, her songs and her stories,
And such tall tales as well. These brightly coloured
Flags of herself.

Comparing and repeating, she eloquently holds your hand.
The smiling mouth smelling of sunshine, painting words.

Weather Report

Cold snaps, fleet moored
Bare branches against dull skies.
General absence of colours, flowers and soft leaves.

Soil freezes, winter rains,
Severe frost, kills shoots.
Vast voids vibrating.

Winter gales swell calm seas,
Then spray springs up.

The chill is short.
But to avoid unfavourable conditions
Stay dormant just a little longer.

February 26th—Saturday

You walked along the tide line, tempest raging,
Ignored the warning signs. You charged into the gale
And the rain came down on us like sheets.

We didn't drown, but
We clung together for you, interminably.
Anchored in care and love to church, home and harbour.

Some loose nets drifted in the doorway, but washed
Away again.

Wading back into the surf
The impact was like a tremendous explosion.
Left us swirling, blinded. Haunted by dreams,
And bewildered

Then you were back again.
The thunder of advancing waves.
The murmur of retreating waves.
How do you banish the scenes from your mind?

Cent Ice

(Yoghurt got more culture than you)

I know weh yuh deh an
I know weh yuh going.
Yuh full a sweet mouth an jigger foot.
Got more mange than me dog, more purr than me cat.

Yuh dutty tribe full a yaws;
All a yuh hang on like a rash an tic.
Friday night yuh ready to drop—licks.
An we did beg yuh fuh stop.

Me blood never tek yuh.
Yuh can't better yuhself wid big eye
Ajoupa people can't live in town
All a yuh family chop people—rob cattle.
Cocksure now. Yuh knock bottle, spoon an pot
Yuh brains like calabash
Guts. All white, no grey matter.
An we did beg yuh fuh stop.

Yuh cut ass, cut tail, yuh pepper she skin;
Yuh buss an lash she.

Well chamar, this is me last word,
So never say yuh never heard,
Cos somebody gon come an show yuh your place,
Somebody gon come an mash up yuh face.

Me family deh quiet now, is so we deh, saying nuttin.
But one day, one day, congotay. We gon ketch yuh
An sit down yuh rass.

We gon learn yuh lil manners. An melt yuh.

The Shoot

She paid $100, put on the powder,
And fixed up her dress.
Then she readjusted the bachelor button on it.
"Na waste time fuh nothing
draw up a chair
I gon draw yuh photo gal."
She took off her red rubber slippers slowly
And put on crepsole shoes.

He said, "Look sharp now, I ready gal."
"Man don't rush me
Or I gon give you piece of me mind.
I done grease yuh hand already."
He said, "Hustle up and
Haul yuh fat ass outa here quick.
Stop titivating like a moo-moo."

Eh, eh, then cut eye start fuh happen:
She said, "You used to eye me up before the buck skin
Gal catch you. I hear she one force ripe piece
Like a feg of orange. Since when you tek magga gal?"

He replied, "Since you look like a manatee."

"Draw me passport photo now. I ready to go."

[She: ASIDE]
"Now I vex bad. I got to wreck yuh up an bruk yuh
    down.
I gon wuk a bad eye on yuh, yuh bharwa, lungeera,
    nimacaram.
Yuh jumbie-boor, yuh gon ketch goady. Yuh maakaa-
    choody.

Soon-soon time yuh gon bawl like barracuda bite yuh
  rass.
Yuh gon glad fuh yuh dead-out even, yuh maakaa-choody.

I gon out yuh light
And yuh rass gon shite."

Non-Divine High

He's a rash of measles
Cocked up like weasel with skunk.

Head down, the old
Shudder, heave and gasp.
He's battled in no man's land for his lump of black.

Here he comes around the bend, lead free
Reared up like bear,
Wide-eyed and pale.

He's careering off the fast track, rudderless.
Onto weed and rubbish covered carpet.
Surreal camaraderie one minute, then 'cool' disinterest.

No *vita nova* for this dejected dope.
Press the eject button on Schubert's songs of loss,
Jettison some controversial scenes.
A decade of deaths, and hopes dashed.

This "Island fortress/garden of England"
Is just a romantic myth.
Homes are awash with spliff,
Billowing.

The Self Help Co-Operative
For D. D.

He said, "Write your thoughts down,
Read 'plotting the narrative' by …………..
Get laid, restart your life,
Buy lots of champagne. Celebrate every day, occasion it;
Don't retard. Go out. Enjoy yourselves.
Tragedy *happens* to siblings. But don't cry too long—cope
   my loves.

[Recover, you emotional skunts.]"

His hair fell like rain. Heavy tears everywhere.
Practised 'chequebook diplomacy'. Hid from us
His pain and grief.
Formally identified his younger sister you know.
Analysis of situation was—conclusion.

Poverty. Words. Work even more.
He sagged with concern.

With glimmers of energy, he dragged himself out of his car
Wearily to Mummy's door. Journey long.
Solid, immovable pain jumped out of his eyes, jabbed his
   skin.
Mourning. Breath checked. Controlled grief.
"Discuss future only. Look at other possibilities."
Blurred tongue he faltered in conversation's flow.
Stress. Key words. Statements. Worried.

"Love of all, for all,
Don't fall anchored in plots."

Bad Lucky Moo-Moo

"I gon dig out yuh eye if yuh tell lie," me mooma say.
She cuss me belly, me ass, back and side complete.
She chase me wid belna with her mouth big,
"Good for yuh, yuh like butter-flap wid man
Now yuh catch belly, news gon spread like fire.
Shame deh on we now.
Yuh say yuh dance calypso wid the cock-eye man?
Good for yuh, man na force yuh …..
It tek 2 hands to clap.
Yuh skin yuh teeth, yuh skin yuh leg
Yuh gon cry soon.
Yuh suck yuh teeth to me so long.
Soon yuh got to push out pickney,
And then yuh gon only skin up yuh mouth and cry.
Suck teeth done now. Pickney got for suck milk."

"Mooma, I never sleep with no rangotang
man. I never show no man me motion.
I tek me rock cake and mauby, sit under the sapodilla tree.
And me fall asleep.
Jumbie must be come and work obeah.
I hear lil soo-soo. I feel like I get nara.
And now … I expectin.

"Mooma. Don't swell up yuh mouth. Just tell all
This is another virgin birth.

"Mooma. Shut yuh mouth before yuh catch fly."

A Morning on the Algarve

In the sun, my shadow lies before me.
Dark impulsive thoughts nose up like submarines.

The drink's what makes the demons dance.
And by lunchtime, they've cloned themselves,
Immerged in vengeance and rhyme.

A handful of sleepless nights, and I see the still born moon
In its coracle
Impaled by arthritis. I tilt the half-moon at will,
And it drowns . . . .
Heart bangs aimlessly as morning floats.

Exuberance is beauty
(after Richard Adams)

Clusters of conkers and
Blackberries and scarlet rose-hips in glowing festoons
Bright as beads or pearls of dew. An array of
Beech, chestnut and oak leaves hanging still. Intricate,
On a maroon October afternoon.

We'll soon have high bouts of wind at Hallowe'een.
They'll moan, sucking in and spitting out.
Then a pelting down of rain and some snow in storms.

And all will be gone like a tourist crowd
From a market town.

Sound of water, smell of sodden leaves.
Fallow deer everywhere.
Redbreast sings, asserting himself, claiming his patch
In short, sweet-toned phrases.

Big spiders clamber and claw in hedges
And smaller ones twine in long grass below.

Limbs exposed, leafless shapes of trees appear,
Trunks glistening in the rain. Bare braches slap each other
In chilling yellow sunset sky. Days sinking, night digging in.

But wait for the magical Holly. She is not barren and drowsy.
See her, beaming,
Mourning not for the end of day.
With blood-red berries and evergreen crisp curling leaves
She braves frost, snow and storm.
Like stars, her balls and baubles hang.

Spiritual Ascension
(for Paul Nicholas Niland)

Palm trees and poinsettia hedges fringe the airport at Faro.
The sunset on red hills beams dull copper.
House-martins free wheel in a clear sky.
A month to clear the mind.

Music therapy, regain rhythm, smell the wild thyme.
A time to heal and disentangle on lazy pool waves.
Nostalgia, whimsy, wistful daze.

Casa Guymara: a place of ceaseless human inactivity.
Lambs graze surrounded by glistening olive groves,
While rabbits race.

Bustle in Loulé market place. Fish lying
In heaps on slabs. Noise and smells galore.

Orchards, grapevines, oranges and pomegranate flower.
And then from sunny Portugal to

Shady Surrey, suddenly.
But this is
Contentment.
The milk of Paradise drunk.
Memories embalmed forever.

E-Mail To God

To: God@hotmail.com
From: Orinoco_Online@lycos.co.uk
Subject: Bless me Father for I have sinned ...
Date: 01/01/01

I'm a little scared of sending this, because you might
Reply one of these days.
I'm sorry I flooded your message board
But I'm scared and losing my faith.

There's no comfort in prayer. No hope.
I see you as frightening and remote.
A figure of judgement and retribution,
I feel no sense of absolution.

Doubt resides in my foundation
You've abandoned me, without salvation.

Where is the caring arm?
The shepherd's crook
For this lost lamb?

Please don't forsake me
I do still try

Please help
Yours truly,

Orinoco_Online

_____

The e-mail has been scanned for honesty and has been
certified cliché free.